WHERE ROOTS ECHO

Where Roots Echo

For Trip and Men –

Mary Caskey

Hope you like these poems –
Love –
Mary Caskey

WIND PUBLICATIONS

International Standard Book Number   978-1-893239-62-3
Library of Congress Control Number   2007933750

First Edition

Acknowledgments

My thanks to the editors of the following journals in which these poems have previously appeared:

Chiron Review — "A Morning with a Friend"
The Christian Science Monitor — "Vermont Country Stores," "When You Call Me"
Connections — "Concentration," "Spring Returns"
Earth's Daughters — "Thank God It's You," "It's Harder to Play these Days"
Grasslands Review — "When Your Mind"
Korone — "Storm Survivor," " On Losing an Oak"
The Mid-America Poetry Review — "Survivors," "Irish Wisdom," "Two Perspectives"
Milkweed Editions, *Stories from Where We Live: The Great Lakes* — "An Evening on Isle Royale"
Moon Journal — "Observing an Opossum," "Puttering," "A Message to the United States"
Powhatan Review — "When Poppies Open in the Snow," "A Question of Shape," "I Have a Private Lair," "Musings"
Prairie Wind — " When Poppies Open in the Snow"
The Rockford Review — "Achilles' Tail," "Camp Fuller," "The Pitchfork's There," "It All Counts," "Information and Knowledge," "Revisiting my Father's Warehouse"
Rock River Times — "A Message to the United States"
Snowy Egret — "An Evening on Isle Royale," "A Morning in a Blueberry Patch," "On the Coast"

For David

Contents

Falling Short

Learning from Knowledgeable Companions

We Balance in Unison

Private Lairs

I Have a Private Lair

that is as open as the prairies of Kansas,
soft as cashmere goats, deep
as a desert well, a place
where roots echo and wind
blows blue balm on a hopscotching mind,
where sometimes fire crackles,
fields of books bloom, and
a patch of myself greens,
where there is such silence
I can hear lichen on a rock,
the growing ring of a red oak,
a tuft of floating milkweed seeds,
and where sometimes words spring into poems
like water pulsing from a well.

Home's

where there's always an acorn in my pocket
  when oak leaves litter the lawn,
    where I know the rattle in the eaves trough
      is just a chipmunk carrying on

where rain falls in rhythm on the skylight
  through a ladder of ivy glistening with dew,
    where I can spurn an impulse called neatness,
      read instead of cleaning the loo,

where my toes curl into a deep red rug,
  a favorite song is that of a towhee,
    where my breath is in sync with a faucet's drip
      and where a lode of peace runs through me.

Onion, Dear

you master of masquerade,
there you are: round, compact,
dirt-bred, compost fed,
spared even
the tender stroke of a hoe,
clothed in a skimpy tissue,
stolid there in the grocery bin,
layers of wrapped, anemic skin, that's all,
flesh that's shrugged off slugs and grubs
and snubbed the strut of garlic-mustard weed.

But when I bring you home, one cut
and you cuff me on the ear.
You are loud, trumpeting
your odiferous presence,
audacious, like a wasp
arousing tears and stinging eyes,
territorial, smothering hyacinths
and paper whites, powerful enough
to transform noodles
into ragtime jazz.

Why I'm Ambivalent About Taking Pictures

I crawl on hands and knees
    to the lowest windows of the porch
        determined not to notify

the feeding titmouse of my presence.
    I can feel my knees creak as I crouch
        to get a straight angle on my grandson.

I ignore the mosquito near my right ear
    to catch the light just right
        entering an opening rose.

Once a friend drove across town
    to get a cumulous cloud
        when it passed over the church,

and another waited two hours
    for a groundhog to stick his nose
        out of his den.

It's possible to have no distinct memory
    of conversation with a dear daughter
        at an important family occasion

because catching the light on her hand,
    the crooked smile, a tilted chin
        was unexpectedly elusive.

The camera's a dilemma:
    moments moments moments
       lost in shooting a picture

that will never be just right,
    yet, there's the photo,
       an instant of lean reality preserved.

Retirement

"I'll never quit work.
Whatta you do
with all that time?" — a friend

Yes, the photos
are sorted,
attic organized
alphabetically,
house repainted
though carpenter ants
still ratchet the roof.
You think I'm a sloth,
sleep till ten every day,
lunch with my wife?
Sure, the gardens are weedless,
and yea, the rumor
that I'm building a birch bark canoe
is correct,
and I do spend whole afternoons
photographing flying squirrels
nibbling nasturtiums.
Tomorrow
I have a colonoscopy,
across the road
from my sometime-womb,
Barnes and Noble,
where I own a slice
of the history shelves.
Once in a while, I hope

the wife's still on errands
when I come home,
and some nights, it's true,
I can't find anything
to crow over.
Just remember: I have time
to canoe the Congo,
slalom in the Olympics, and
I don't have to wear
a watch.

Mid January

I laugh at myself
as I drive the car twenty yards
to bring in the newspaper, inch
baby steps down the sidewalk,
decline once-treasured
moonlit walks, squawk at neighbors
who don't clear their sidewalks,

but the truth is ice,
once prized for beauty and fun,
has become a traitor, lying in wait
under fresh snow, as silent as a panther,
its presence often as unknown
as the day of your death,
its effect when it catches you
sudden and merciless: one skid
and you crumble.

Nothing used to beat swinging
over the creek on our weeping willow,
the ice a showering shimmer,
crackling like musketry hitting the ground;
or sliding down the biggest Sinnissippi hill
aiming for maximum skid and thrill;
or ice skating out on the Rock River
after one brave father has tested
to be sure it is safe.

Today I choose a book and an easy chair
looking out on ice that's basted

the naked branches of the perfect trees,
that glitters on the evergreen's baubles
and on the stalactites hanging from eaves,
all the while watching embers in the fireplace
and fading now and then into another world.

Puttering

waits like a hibernating raccoon
for the weekend that follows
long days at work.

It stretches its tentacles slowly
Saturday morning, basting a list-driven mind
like the warm water of an evening bath.

It is a grain of yeast
inside a rising loaf of bread,
the red bob at the end of a fish line
treading water,
an earthworm
aerating subterranean soil.

A day of puttering is a prize,
a massage for the brain,
a day when even the marrow of your bones
stops shouting directions.

Kinds of Refreshment

I'm sitting on a sagging basswood bench
overlooking a whaling village,
a rail fence blocking my view
(I'm short) but ensuring
     I don't fall off the precipice.

Together we've just loaded dirty laundry
into the only public washing machine
in town. You counted out the required
Canadian coins even though you'd hardly noticed
     we were out of clean socks.

Now, what to do in this remote camping ground
while the machine does its work? You opt
for a nap, scrunching up your knees
on the Toyota's back seat. I choose
     this sagging bench, paper, and pen.

When we emerge from our reveries,
fold each piece of underwear
and admit to each other that, yes,
cleanliness is next to godliness,
     we are both fresher.

The Red Boat Cushion

I pull weeds
                out of each crevice
                in a brick sidewalk,
like a rabbit at work.
I'd rather be reading a book.

My seat is a red boat cushion
that's been around
                the Great Lakes
                for fifty years,
lost its fire-engine hue
exudes gray kapok
                but has lumps
                of such comfort

that I invite
                Captain Ahab
                and Ernest Hemingway
to share my other two red cushions
and swill dandelion wine.

Musings

Sometimes when I see
the frenzy of Japanese beetles,
swarming, gorging on pink wild roses
so fast the petals fall to the ground,
I wonder what happens to these creatures.
    Do their green metallic heads ever rest
    on bronzed wings in bliss?

Sometimes when I see my husband's head sink
into the crook of an arm,
his eyes close like those of a china doll's,
breathing heavy, breath slow,
I cheer the peace of sleep,
    soothing as a silky wave,
    cool and blue as a gulf breeze.

Other times when I watch his head sink,
I think of the final fading
out of a body, away from the castle
of verbenum that grows by the window,
away from the solid oaks and carpets of ivy,
    and I'm all right: just being part
    of the continuum of things

It All Counts

When the flat light of morning
strikes the top of winter's naked trees,
hear the hum of your orange squeezer
the sizzle of bacon in the skillet blackened
by years on a grandma's hearth,
the drill of a downy woodpecker chiseling
his suet sacrament at your window sill.
Breathe in your best beloved's
minty toothpaste, his hair
anointed with shampoo, and
mark the milk that
drips slightly from his chin
when he looks up from the journal
straight into your eyes.

Note the double exposures that dip
in and out of your head: times
meandering through orange blossoms
south of Tampa, frying pans
over outdoor coals, sink shampoos
and vinegar rinses, autumn's
giant evening shadows,   so that
when you return to the chapel
that is your stove,
you'll welcome Vesta
who's just popped in
to bless your hearth.
Sail her a wafer, fill her vessel with tea
and baptize the missal she brings
that lets you know it all counts.

Feeling Cobblestones

Advice for the Italian Traveler

After the drama of the duomo's
black and white marble
and the bliss of quiet in its chapel,
seek out a bench in the village piazza
and tune in as though you'll never be there again.
Hear fingers froth the fountain, syncopated jazz
in a game of tag, lilts in a Mama's monologue,
the pounding feet of soccer tilts. Float
with baking bread, browning pizza, lemon lilies,
feel cobblestones under your bare soles,
the tingle of each sip of wine.

And take particular note of the graffiti
when you spend the evening in Siena's piazza:
"sei no credi a soigni sei morto,"
is scrawled on the shabby shingles
of a shuttered, outdoor market,
"If you don't believe in dreams,
                         you're dead."
Wonder about this Italian scrawler,
an Artemesia, perhaps, a Catherine or Clare;
hover around the market tomorrow,
happen upon her and catch her eye.

Taormina

When the deep blue Ionian sea is so clear
you can see the color of each stone
and feel its sensuous smoothness
on the lava-lined bottom,
when the touch of a kayak paddle
to the blue is as silent
as the tuna who swims below,
when the morning sunlight turns a cruiser
in the harbor into a Phoenician galley,

reach for the hand of the man beside you
who is sipping his caffe macchiato
and who may be seeing just water
and a big boat   or who may be feeling
the fingers of Zeus on his shoulder.
In the clasp are marinating threads
that weave you to the past and
to your steady voyage
toward the painted island you both can see.

Crossing the Straits

You know from eighth grade mythology
that Charybdis will suck either you
or the nearby swordfishermen
into her whirlpool,
or, alternatively,
that a monster
named Scylla
will eat you
in the depths
that is the water
there near Messina
where you ferry to Sicily
on a green boat named Archimedes,
the knowledge drowning, once and for all,
your steady, heron-like faith in water's balm.

A Question of Shape

Sicily
ought to be round
instead of triangular
to celebrate its oranges
which grow to become globes
thriving in the rich black lava soil
so flawless there are no seeds and
so juicy they are fountains under your tongue.
Sicily ought to be round to honor black olives
so piquant their nip incises your palate,
so prolific they must be caught in nets
as they fall from gray, contorted trees,
silver like the tuna off this island
that ought to be round,
not triangular,
Sicily.

The Mystery of Capers

When you come upon a caper bush
growing out of the wall of an abbey
somewhere in eastern Sicily
in a rain so gentle
it barely bastes the plant,

when you see its sleek white petals
blaze with masses
of purple-tipped filaments
that remind you
of Door County ladyslippers,

you'll be surprised to hear
the distress of the Mother Abbess
at the ripening blossom,
you'll wonder why its natural beauty
is not an object of her worship,

until she tells you
in a pedagogical, botanical voice
that caper bushes are valuable
only for their buds
which must be nipped and pickled,

an elegant salty condiment,
without which tonno griglio,
for example, would be incomplete:
a sacrifice of beauty
for the palate.

The Cotswolds

Once in England in the Cotswolds
we tramped from Upper to Lower Slaughter,
towns along the trail of Warden's Way
where sheep by the thousands
once grazed among clumps of grass
and lichened limestones: grand, square
animals, with dense, pure white wool,
known through Europe as Cotswold lions.

In the distance we saw manor houses,
castles, and golden row cottages,
once home to weavers, shearers, and shepherds,
the roofs boldly gabled and steeply pitched,
swallows nesting in the dormers.
Limestone walls laced the land,
horizontal stones, each placed
for balance without Atlas or mortar.

Turnstiles separated one neighbor's field
from the next, the gate like an entrance
to a subway until we caught the scent
of marjoram and wild thyme,
heard the monotone of bees, and saw
the imprint of hooves, beech trees,
and the careless snooping
of a blue butterfly.

Today there are few sheep. When we stopped
on a stony outcropping, their bodies,
even the white ribbon of their forelocks,
didn't move. Only brown eyes,
trusting as open-faced flowers, followed us.
They and the ancient manor houses
were as silent and as grand
as a pasture of northern lights.

Return to Sanibel

I.

When I sat on the bench in the darkness,
my only sense of place
the steady lap of waves on shore,

>   I was uncertain for a moment
>   of where I was,
>   a zinnia in a new bed,

>   until an orange moon, one night past full,
>   pulled out of a cloud, like a dolphin
>   gliding out of waves along the shore

and I could see the silhouette of a familiar palm
and its offshoot, looking like a piliated woodpecker:
I knew I was back again, and rooted.

II.

While I watch the male osprey,
crouched in the crook of a dead pine,
overlooking the harum-scarum nest
he has built twig by twig
on the same Sanibel platform
that has been his home for years
with the same female who curls up now
on the soft weeds that are her contribution,
when I see him nudge their chick

and open his wings teaching a law
of aerodynamics, when the threesome
are still there after last night's big wind,
I think of my husband.

III.

Floating into the gulf
on an inflated, red, rubber raft,
one ear at rest on a pillow of puff,

> the gulls and I confronting the wind,
> tufts sleeked by breeze and surf,
> I'm a sunscreened log just set adrift

> hoping the neighborhood baby dolphin
> will cross my path and give me a nuzzle.
> It's not just my body floating away,

my thoughts are drifting too:
hush-a-bye, baby, the water's warm,
softly, softly the waves are basting;
the owl and the pussy-cat beckon me on.

Nancy's

is the last stop before Sanibel,
down a dirt road decked
with plastic pelicans and terns, past clumps
of crab grass leading to stumps
that are markers for parking.

It's a freshly painted green shack
with an earthen floor, eaves that droop,
a weathered roof that sags and sprouts
mesh bags of grapefruit, braids of garlic,
and sacks of oranges holding down

a red, white and blue flag that proclaims
the place is open. Lopsided signs
announce the latest Georgia pecans,
blue-ribbon key lime pie, lordly grapefruit,
honey bonbons and jumbo boiled peanuts.

Nancy, gray and weathered too,
sits cross-legged behind the counter
polished by thirty years of hard work,
her smile the shack space heater,
her language citrus and cash.

Vermont Country Stores

No neon sign nor great marquee,
just a clothesline
of hand-sewn quilts
announces these emporiums
where usually
the owner's dog
nuzzles your elbow
while your arms
reach out
to an array of goods
as crowded as an acre of corn
and as compact as a hardware drawer:
maple syrup, fudge slabs,
village maps, knickknacks,
wood stacks
and cat-shaped dog biscuits
near which the nose
of the fellow at your elbow
grows more insistent.

You may not be a shopping fan
but where there's a country store
    whose owner hums
and whose dog thanks
with enormous and gentle eyes,
    you'll be around.

Vermont

When the innkeeper bows you
    into the parlor,
peopled with drop-leaf tables and copper pots,
    settle in
with the latest Times, a glass of wine,
    your feet up

until the daily dinner fest
    for which this wizard
has hired a licensed forester
    to root for mushrooms
which he offers tonight
    with quail, venison, goose

along with summer squash
    and the bloom of a nasturtium
that tops your salad in the shade
    of your costume,
all the while wielding
    bellows and whisk broom,

lugging logs and questioning guests
    shall we or shall we not
light a fire this evening
    and don't you like
my latest Rockwell print?

And, yes, with another set of fingers,
    he's combing the library
for the newest tome on covered bridges
    and mapping a route
to your trail tomorrow
    and the closest stream for trout.

In the morning he piles your plate
    with scones and cakes.
It's likely by then you'll think
    he made the moon last night
and morning's slant of sunshine
    on your arm.

A Morning in a Blueberry Patch

There is a sharp climb up from the bay
to low shrubs, junipers, gray rock
where blueberry bushes grow competing
with gray-green and orange lichen, sure signs
the air is as pure as Annapurna's.

We'd beached the canoe on stone slabs
and tied it to a white spruce. Even close to the water
there were blueberries, blue gold, and
as we fanned out, we could hear
the first berries hit the bottom of our buckets.

Every once in a while, we'd find a patch so prolific
we'd gasp, kneel, and set down our buckets
to pick with both hands, offering silent thanks
that there are no bears on Isle Royale,
stepping gingerly, always on the lookout

for the scat of moose. Stillness is punctuated
by clack of grasshoppers and drone of bumblebees,
this island's only versions of a jet boat. The cool
of the water soothes our scratched hands as we
spread our lunch on a canoe paddle,

sit on cushions of moss and lichen, sip
apple juice, peel oranges, and tune
to a mother loon who's giving diving lessons,
five baby ducks swimming around our canoe,
and the prospect of fresh, warm blueberry pie.

Oceanic

The worn gray log, our picnic bench,
matched the sky that day in July
when the Pacific, at football field's distance,
was just a simmer, its downy waves
kissing cormorants and tickling
two red-throated loons

skipping and skimming the water,
which lured me, and I was up
walking past our halcyon perspective,
past the high tide watermark, close enough
to hear only the roar of waves,
hard harsh pounding water at rolling boil.

Vapor steamed above the seething shadow side
of this stretch of ocean, concealing the vultures
in its undertow, the fisticuffs
in its turbulence, the treason in its grandeur,
its seductive, softening collapsed waves
a thin veil separating gentleness and rage.

On the Coast

At the edge of the cliff,
the path dotted with wild iris,
blue-eyed grass, goldfinch
and Douglas swallows who swooped
like maypole dancers,
we expected an uninhabited cove,

quiet as a northwoods pond.
The first signs it would be otherwise
were soft cries and the stench
of tenement sea life, and then below,
a colony of harbor seals,
sunning on rocks like Rorschach blots.
Their barrel bodies,

mottled gray or spotted black,
stretched, slept, clambered
for footholds, slipped in slime.
At the cove entrance a bearded one
swam lengths, the shark patrol,
while babies struggled

to reach a mother's teat,
their short legs useless
against kelp-strewn rock
and pounding tide, their only grace
slow slides and dives to the sea:
a village of languid creatures
polishing another generation.

Falling Short

An Angler Meets John Locke

Once when I was a new bride, I jumped
at the chance for a 10 pm fishing excursion
with the man I loved calling husband
after a day of being a "good guest"
at the cottage home of his uncle.

There was, of course, a moon on the water
and stars brighter than we'd ever see in town.
He tied on my favorite plug, a gray mouse
whose paint was chipped but whose silken
thread of a black tail was still soft

in my fingers as I stroked it
for good luck before I cast the mouse
into thick, tangled, gauze-green weeds
off Forbes' point, where just the day before
an otter had been playing.

Our fishing record was a family joke:
if you counted the cost of the gear
and the license and divided that sum
by the number of fish we caught
in a year, we were losing,

so when a smallmouth bass swallowed
the hook of my mouse and dove down
through the weeds, when he jumped
as I reeled, when my husband netted

a prize-sized bass on the first try,
my mind had already leapt to a taxidermist.
But I didn't have a chance to measure
or weigh my prize because the love of my life
threw the fish back in: "The season doesn't open

for two hours," he said. "I don't think
that fish is ours." That's the story:
it's become family lore, worth a good laugh
at least once each summer since that fish
swam away more than fifty years ago

and a good reminder (as he told me that night
after I calmed down) of the social contract
we all freely enter and of my continuing respect
for the husband whose gentle voice
helped hone my way of making choices.

Insufficiencies

I used to park behind the library beside the river
where it curves under the Jefferson Street bridge
and where there were plenty of spaces
right at nine and no major street to cross.
A stooped and empty-handed man always stood

at the entrance waiting for the doors to open,
warmth to seep through his ragged blue jeans,
the chance to pee in a bathroom and splash
cold water on a face so hidden by gray and greasy hair
that only his blood-rimmed blue eyes were visible.

My daughter, a social worker, has told me
not to look away: he is too used to being ignored,
looked through as though he were a Pompeian statue.
I'd wish I'd remembered to pack
a ham and cheese sandwich instead of

half a smile. These days I park in the lighted lot
in front of the library, walk in with down-coated,
ear-muffed, sightless manikins. The chestnut
that I used to massage in my pocket
for solace, I clutch these days for falling short.

It's Harder to Play These Days

when even the weather
is running amuck, earth warmer,
columbines blooming in February,
swallows heading north
in what we used to call winter
and further afield
fewer emperor penguins,
the snows of Kilimanjaro almost gone.
I try to stay tuned, still,
to the continuing voices of our woods:
a loquacious squirrel,
the beating wings of a red-tailed hawk,
a cardinal's chirp at dawn,
sounds I've known since I was a girl
in these same woods,
then streaking in and out of the trees,
playing capture the flag, kick the can, hide and seek.
I remember being "it:"
safeguarding the goal, daring to inch out
intent as a mother chickadee
tuned to the rustling of leaves,
the crack of a branch, a scuttling chipmunk,
the caw of a crow, eyes vigilant
like a loon watching her brood.
There were eight of us
who knew every fallen tree trunk,
every patch of nettles, every stump in the woods,
and we were free as gazelles in the grassland,
wild as a single poppy in a meadow,
carefree as romping pups.

Desolation Sound, British Columbia

September 11, 2001

We paddled Desolation Sound
when New York skies turned gray
and quests for peace were drowned.

It was coincidence that we found
ourselves in a kayak that fateful day
paddling Desolation Sound

where what we heard was the pound
of Kwakiutl drums in ceremonial play,
their quest for peace not drowned

though in New York two towers were downed,
three thousand people fell, prey,
while we paddled Desolation Sound

in flags of kelp our paddles bound.
New York flags were burned and frayed;
their quest for peace was drowned.

The Tower site's now sacred ground;
Kwakiutls continue to pray
paddling Desolation Sound,
the quest for peace not drowned.

A Message to the United States

from Wiliam Oltetia, June, 2002

Though you do not know me,
I know you: I heard
of your September calamity
when winter was near in Kenya
and it was spring in the USA.
I am a wandering Masai,
cattle raiser, tender of acacia trees
and the giraffes that eat their leaves.

I've seen a radio and a TV,
but I learn most from storytellers
like Kimeli, who is learning
to be a doctor in your country
and came home last week
to tell us of the fall of the towers.

Listening, we could feel the fire of your pain,
the endless black trenches of your losses,
the rough reefs of your wounds,
the desert of your grief.
We are unable to imagine buildings so high
a person who had to jump would die.

Today, my village dressed
in red tunics and painted necklaces
to bless fourteen of our cows.
We danced and chanted
around these sacred animals

as we have done for generations;
but this time an American flag
rested on the shoulder of our leader,

for these cows we give to you.
They are the marrow of our bones,
our daughters' dowries;
we can do no less.
May only our faces
be invisible to you.

Weekend in Assisi

When I was small, I loved to hear
the stories of St. Francis,
so I held my breath as though
embarking on a long crusade
when we arrived on Mt. Subasio,
listening for the Saint's own lark,
stepping on Assisi's square

where narrow lanes led down
to patios of lemon vine,
tiers of clay-tiled roofs,
and window boxes for both
flower beds and clothes lines,
where tiny plots of yard were havens
for peace lilies and for roses
and where from Rocca Maggiore
poppies tattooed miles of green.

Gelato bars, outdoor cafes,
music, shoppers, sippers, browsers
filled the fountained square,
while Franciscan friars
in brown robes and cowled shawls
with belts of cord and rough hewn thongs
were glimpsed within the church
blending with Giotto's work.

Sunday, the piazza was silent:
no hawking peddlers, clink of wares,
only crowds around a kiosk
staring at *Le Stampe's* headline:
"Falcone dead: a Mafia deed;"
he who was Italian justice,
prosecutor of corruption,
gone, victim of a bomb.
We who were that day's Assassins,
mourners all, signed petitions,
listening for a lark.

Learning From Knowledgeable Companions

An Evening on Isle Royale

At dusk we watched
a moose forage
for a cache of salad
in a swampy bog
close to Hidden Lake
where old-timers insist
you go if you haven't
yet happened on the goal
of every Isle visitor: moose.

Her brown hulk
trapped the last rays
of sunlight against a crowd
of balsam deadheads,
her forelegs were splayed
like a giraffe's, and the dangling
bell of her throat just
skimmed the water.
When she lifted her long face,

green lilies dripped from her chin.
The distance between us
was so short
we could see the majesty
of her brown mass,
the veil of her shyness,
a carnival of an appetite,
and enormous joy in the long full snort
that dismissed our presence.

Observing an Opossum

Drop everything when you see her
lumber down the pavement of your driveway
just as daytime breezes die to a whimper
and the first star blinks in blue-black sky.

Drink in her pale white face, a mask
of an ancient ghost, and her long nose, naked ears,
pink prehensile tail. Pick up your binoculars
to see her marsupial pouch: discover at least
twelve tiny creatures jostling for a teat,
in this, their castle for the first twelve weeks.
Watch their mother hunt eggs, berries, mice;
imagine her cumbered climb each night
to a leaf-lined hole in a nearby oak. Keep an eye out
at dusk: witness those babes, now older
and strong enough to hold on to their mother's tail,
a muscle, her fifth arm, their wagon.

Imagine rubbing a hand over the coarse hairs
that are her fur; don't scare her: she'll freeze.
Try imitating her trudge; soak in the long trail
of her instincts and the colony that rides on her tail.

Twin Fawns

One morning in June, twin fawns
who live in the denseness of our woods
ventured close enough so I could count
the white dots of the stripes

that mark their backs,
see the nubbins of white down
behind their knees, watch a long tongue
reach back to lick a flank, ears recline

at the bark of a neighbor's dog,
the paper-white undersides
of six-inch russet tails, and
their straight unbowed front legs.

When they moved even closer,
I could see the tentativeness of their rummagings,
their disdain as they passed over garlic mustard weed
and their relish in a chew of giant hosta

until, recharged, they chased each other
around overgrown junipers,
tore through dewy, glistening grass
in rococo frolic, pas de deux.

Survivors

Two deer kneel,
sink in new snow,
parentheses. Their gaze
never wavers, and hours later
they still stare, necks steady,
sightlines straighter than radar,
meditating yogis,
giving themselves to the earth.

. . . .

Even in the cold
there is joy in our back yard:
nuthatches chisel suet,
goldfinches vie for thistle seed,
squirrels squabble for leftovers,
a junco steams in the bird bath,
crows blaze, a Downy squeaks...here
where only tracks tattoo the snow,
icicles are silent, evergreens rigid,
and even the neighborhood cat
has stayed at home.

. . . .

I see movement in the woods:
out through the kitchen window,
out past the birdbath, a deer rises from the snow,

the outline of her form in the first light of dawn
as stark as the naked trunk of a tree.
She stretches her neck upward, searching
a green oasis, then lowers
her nose to snow and frozen weeds.
Fading into the forest, she turns, and
her ribs are visible in each step;
her belly is large. Will there be two
to savor summer birch?

Storm Survivor

She doesn't seem to miss the swimmers:
bronzing girl in white maillot
or the fat woman in black
who holds her knees together
when she jumps into the pool.

She doesn't miss
the coconut oil and Coppertone and
she doesn't seem to notice that
even the trunks of the palms
bend in the wind.

Her step is as measured and slow
as the Queen of England's;
she stands occasionally
on one of her reedy legs,
self-conscious and attentive.

The heron is the only one
at the pool
in gusts of wind
so fierce the hairs of her white crown
stand up like bulrush spikes.

The Heron

The heron on the other bank of the pond
is searching for breakfast, yellow eyes intent,
yellow bill steady, body alert,
tensed for a quick grab
of the first available floating insect.
Neither the ring of a cellphone, exclamation points
in a voice, or a competitive seagull overhead
interrupt his concentration.
He isn't disturbed by the shimmering trees
in the water nor stymied
by the pond's thick algae.
I admire the fire of his determination,
the clear liquid of his vision,
the rock of his concentration.
I don't always know how to pick
among the multitude of choices
along the path,
but I do know
I'm quite taken
with the heron on the other bank of the pond.

The Sea Otter

rested on her back, paws so relaxed
they dangled like a spaniel's ears
near where the pool at the zoo
curved closest to the pedestrian pier.
"Catching her breath," we said
having watched her calypso antics
slithering down a twisting muddy slide,
arms tucked into her side, a yogic
cobra pose, short legs and long tail
streaming behind, eyes closed,
whiskers drooped. She was as oblivious
to the world, we thought, as we grow
when on vacation   until she turned her head,
opened a mocha eye, and winked.

Spring Returns

The first sign the towhees were back
was a small disturbance in the underbrush:
scattering dried leaves and dirt caught my eye,
but the brown of the female blended with the ground
so that I almost missed seeing the bird.

Earlier, in pouring rain and a green slicker
Norah had brought two pink plastic bags
bursting with mertensia. "It's a good day
for digging," she'd said, and so you and I donned
black waterproof pants, rubbers, windbreaker,

and headed off into the woods. Spring had come
and although we dropped down on our knees as always
to touch aconite and the pink buds of spring beauties
just poking through lingering patches of snow,
though we lovingly patted the black earth

around the newly planted mertensia, this year we were bound,
jaws set, to defeat an enemy: garlic mustard weed,
a phalanx of plants so thick, fertile, voracious it threatens
to take the place of our beloved wildflowers,
glistening euonymous, ivy, and pachysandra.

The attack: pulling out each weed by the roots,
muddy, pungent, clumpy, then keeping at it
despite the distraction of goldfinch and chickadees,
a raucous crow, sounds of a distant train,
the unending drip of rain through the trees.

The day's accomplishment: eight bags of weeds,
and then, while a male cardinal whistled,
finding on the now bare, beautiful black earth,
a white trillium just breaking through the ground
and two resurrected, craning earthworms.

On Losing an Oak

There are buds
on the fallen tree,
an inch of new life,
though the trunk
that bore that life
has been decapitated
by a guillotine
wind.

It's taking
seven men
to bring that tree
to rest:
*"That old girl is
 heavy now"*
seven men, a crane,
claws, rope, saws
seven men who don't
    see the buds.

Achilles' Tail

Sometimes there is a squirrel alarm in our forest.
You have to stop stock still in your tracks
and concentrate, eyes open,
on the first branches of the thicket

as though you were alone in a jungle
where even the wave of a branch is a signal.
You won't, however, see any monkeys.
It's the tails of the squirrels that'll catch your eye.

In alarms their torsos are totally still
but the tails cannot be suppressed;
they bobble, swish, they've a life of their own
attached to a body, but separate,

a quivering muscle, alive, irrepressible,
brown and bushy, supple and massaged
by the wind, this essence of a squirrel
broadcasts his hiding place.

The Power of Suet

One small cake of suet
in a barred green metal square
looking like a little jail
hangs outside the kitchen window,
its sunflower seeds, millet, lard
and ground corn
manna
for the red-breasted nuthatch
who, upside down, pokes at the cake,
and feast for a red-bellied woodpecker
whose sharper bill makes larger dents,
scattering morsels on the ground
where they are quickly consumed by an envious,
(and obviously intelligent) squirrel.

Inside we who grumble at a dirty cake of suet
replacing blooming purple fuchsia
and hosta spikes with glassy icicles
find the silliness of the nuthatch's mask,
the jauntiness of the woodpecker's crimson cap
softening our edges and easing us
down the long white avenue of winter.

Swamp Stakes

They were yearlings:
you could tell
because the bands that marked
the hide of the alligator's back
were light
and the tip of the heron's beak
was black.

The little heron leaned
toward the alligator's snout
from a limb too fragile
for a ladybug,
the morning still, the pond
disturbed just where the branch
sank under the heron's weight
and by the shadow
of the hawk that flew above.

The heron yawped, then stalled
and waded out, a yogic swan,
to take up watch
two yards away
from the alligator's iron tail
and gawk,
or did she mock?

You couldn't tell
if it was cat and mouse
or hide and seek,

or if so soon
the game had turned
to war.

Information and Knowledge

When I walked to the mailbox this morning
to pull out the daily newspapers, I felt
the load of yet another barrage of information,
grim, complicated facts from all over the world.

But the tremolo of a nesting wren was rescue,
itself like a lark's violin, and a trigger
of two memories from yesterday: chipmunks
in a sexual rumpus through a labyrinth
of red bleeding heart and a small spotted fawn
who'd meandered down our gravel driveway
sampling blue, green, and white-striped hosta
with the quiet assurance of the Dalai Lama.

I was walking in the footsteps of that fawn,
near the flowery maze, a serenade overhead,
learning from my knowledgeable companions.

On a Walkway

One spring on a walkway through palm and oak,
clumps of Spanish moss caught my eye,
drooping, dirty gray like the cement floor in our garage
bedraggled as Rip Van Winkle's beard
brittle like Chinese noodles,
while at the top of an oak
a mockingbird poured forth a non-stop song
as dazzling as sunshine on Caribbean waters
groomed like a coloratura soprano
tender as a letter to a lover,
and though nothing in the world had changed
something inside me stilled,
there on a walkway
in the presence of moss and song.

We Balance in Unison

When You Call Me

from somewhere in our long, still house,
I can tell by the hush in your voice
that you aren't calling for help,
don't need a hand lifting a heavy chest
or opening a stubborn jar, because
it's the same voice you used to use
while you watched our babies
sleeping in their cribs
or when we walk in Severson Dells
searching the earth for wild flowers.
I know when I find you,
you'll reach for my hand.
Last March, I remember
it was the first appearance
of our own long-surviving chipmunk
who wrapped your voice in dew.
Today you've spotted a fawn
who's fallen asleep in the garden.
All three of us breathe in unison.

Thank God It's You

i'd be sponging spots from his tie; that old beau
who used to croon "Bewitched, Bothered, and Bewildered"
is probably befuddled now as well as slow and portly.
i'd be nagging him, too, to hid his dung colored
suspenders under a neutral coat and launching
caustic lances at his crows of old conquests —
while stumbling, he cane-bound, on barnaby's beach.
thank god, it's you beside me now, you beside me
close to fifty years and if i've ever sponged
your spots, it's when you've been so keen on me,
your eyes so clear and doting on me that
you've lost track of your spoon, and there we are,
out of hand, adrift on a peppermint cloud,
sporting sunflower leis, somersaulting in the air.

The Murmansk Hat

He's dubbed it his Murmansk hat; it's better if he owns two
in case one gets lost or is swallowed by the wash.
They're really North Atlantic sailors' caps,
navy, with flaps that pull down over the ears, and a tight weave
that flattens an otherwise handsome head of hair.

He considers this cap his single best investment:
it doesn't show dirt, it's cheap, and it's essential
for a walk to the mailbox, an errand in a cold car,
a windy golf game, emptying the trash, even
the symphony or a fancy party on a January night.

When asked why Murmansk, he talks about a dear uncle
who used to claim he was stationed above the Arctic Circle
during World War II, a navy captain
on the Murmansk run after lurking German subs,
though we all knew he was really on a Greek isle.

On lesser days I fret over the flattened hair;
once I even bought a substitute from L.L. Bean.
More often I like knowing he is warm, and I like
the glint of a good memory in his eye. When I ask him
to ruffle up his hair, "aye, aye, sir" is the reply.

Frolic

When the resident prince of ambrosia
glides around the curve of your chocolate cake,
drop the mop, forget muss,
grab merlot and a parasol,
feel his touch on your elbow
as you lope on out and mount
pogo sticks that sweep you
billowing into the forest glen. There,

where a lone anemone
blooms under sky so Chagall blue
that Keats may come to feast,
where the aura in the air
is of lion and his pride,
and where you needn't heed
the chocolate on your face:
he'll love the taste, there

you'll hear sprites whooping,
earth will rise beneath your bones,
there'll be cellos in his voice so pure
a nightingale may appear,
striking up his own aria
questioning and wondering
if it's only air
that floats between you two.

When Your Mind

is playing cloud hopscotch
and you can't see
blue
pull up a dream
commandeer a cloud
grab your dad

who if you're as old as I
has been gone a while,
but who will remember
your model legs
cool concentration
golden tresses

and who will listen like a musician
supply the answers
to your questions
and the
questions for your
answers because

in his forty years over the moon
he's been feasting on
caviar with Gatsby
catfish with Tom
while swapping lore
with Hemingway

who urged him to come for a day
to dust your clouds

with powdered sugar
sprinkle your lips
with peppermint
your soul with stars

who even as the frost
first fingers
your hair,
smoothes the crow's feet
clears the way
to blue.

A Conversation About a Chair

If the chair, Dad, where I sit today
were still in the house I grew up in,
you'd be watching me in a playpen,
an ashtray with a painted mallard
within reach on the oak, ink-stained desk.

Seems to me the chair had a brown slipcover,
awning cloth with spiraling fall branches,
then later, in our next home, a slippery chintz
rinsed in wild and bold red roses.
Watching from the chintz, you saw me fall in love,

waiting up each night I had a date
to tell us something funny
that you'd gleaned that noon
at Hobson's lunch counter. I knew you too
liked my beau: he still remembers

your head thrown back laughing, yes,
in this very chair, low to the floor, the right height
for you and me, both five-foot-three. It was still chintz
when you, pretty frail, tied those uncomfortable
patent leather shoes to walk me down the aisle.

Well, you knew you could trust me:
the chair's in my house now, different cover,
same old unrefinished feet. Like you,
I write in that chair, and when I find
a gray, curly hair on the cushion, I call it ours.

Revisiting My Father's Warehouse

I like the singleness of standing in stalks of weeds,
thistles, burdock, quack grass, a scrawny brier bush
outside the old red brick warehouse whose name
painted in white block letters near the roof line

is smudged with grime and dimmed by decades of rain.
Its cargo docks are bricked over now, windows
patched with duct tape and cardboard,
railway tracks whose silver once caught

the glint of sunlight mostly gone. Abandoned,
I thought, until I walked around to the Cedar Street
entrance and climbed five black cement stairs
to an office which buzzed me in as it bustled

with business, two computers, fax
and a man named Max, who took me back
into the warehouse to see its massive support cylinders,
patched gray plaster, red brick walls, oily cement floor.

I like the freshness of the current business;
but it's in the solitude of the weeds,
in the mystery of the tracks that I hear
the textured train whistle of the past.

Camp Fuller

Each year in May he hung a thick
braided rope from an old oak tree
that stood in our back yard,
and while we swung, lilacs bloomed.
We'd close our eyes, swing forth,
and hear his voice,

his story now almost a myth,
a chronicle of Rockford men
who'd trained in sixty-two
when Lincoln called "To Arms, To Arms,"
and General Fuller chose the camp
a mile from the center of town
in a tract of oaks, Churchill's grove,
near the Rock River.

We swung, he said, my sister and I,
on earth once scuffed by marching feet
that drilled for General Grant's campaigns,
on earth where tents and barracks sprang,
where women stitched a marathon,
three hundred blues in thirty hours
and farmers hauled their dew-fresh crops,
the wagon loads a traffic jam
upon the river cowpath,
where bands marched, and flag pageants
were just as routine as the scrub
of tin cups, enameled pots,
where the Ladies Aid Society

packaged dressings, passed out Bibles,
hemmed the sheets and pillow cases,
turned the season's berries into jam.

Swing forth, swing back.
The oak tree now is gone.
The rope is dust
and the homestead sold.
But the storyteller's voice remains
like the wooden flute a granddad played
in the Grand Army of the Republic.

The Friendship of Women

Once a year they gather around a well-set table
where it's apparent the hostess has thought for weeks
    about the polishing of silver,
    the mirrored centerpiece,
    the choice of menu:
it's their magic hour of the holiday,
think lights and tinsel and ribboned hair,
a Saturnalia, when the rest of the world blurs.
    Chatter begins when they step
    through the door, mouths move
    faster than feet, breath is on hold,
all five framed by burning candles,
the echo of laughter, oohs and ahs
over pears poached in cranberry juice,
plump, red like burgeoning bows of chiffon
    encircling the women
    sparkling
    in the company of one another.

Mother

We can't resist
an occasional pea,
averted eyes,
did the other see?
newsprint between us
saucepan our altar
beneath a Chinese elm

where every June
we shelled these pearls
fingering each green gem
small round smooth,
nourished in green pods
as shielding as
mud bank wombs
to salmon eggs
or space to stars,

our motion cadenced,
plunks in the pan,
heads close
four freckled hands
    pea and pod.

Irish Wisdom

Today, while I eat a potato
        breaking from the belly of its skin

I'm an opening nasturtium
        in gawky pose, back in time
        in a potato field with Mother.

We balance in unison on shoulders of pitchforks
        and count each ingot of muddy gold
        in the furrows that stretch out ahead.

The Cross

"Don't fret ," she'd said in her motherly voice,
"it'll last even past my death; I nailed it together
in three days, the cross-beam the toughest."
So I didn't need to ask what she thought

about the Aldersgate wooden cross
framed by ruler-straight evergreens against the sky
outside the single window of the small room
that for four years had been her home.

The bed, dresser, and the chair by her side
that I occupied had been in the family for years;
we'd often spend afternoons chatting and listening
to old tunes like Let Me Call You Sweetheart

with one eye on the cross, she in bed, ribs so fragile
one had broken when she raised a plate,
memory so aeronautic the names of her spouses
had flown, and she'd forgotten what to call

her daughters and that her version of a sermon
used to be the song of a cardinal, a chickadee,
her worship roasting potatoes and tenderloin beef
and a walk among sturdy oaks.

She'd been the one who sold the business,
made reservations, arranged the furniture,
decided when it was time to move. I should have known
she'd have a theory about that cross she saw each day.

Gently Through the Clouds

Gently through the clouds that are her mind
she is saying in a quiet voice
that although she is poised
on an unfolding nasturtium,

though she knows
her roses are coned,
burning bushes hushed,
sapling pines mulched,

that though a blackbird on her shoulder
has said today's the day
and she sees light
near where she lies,

though the geography of her face
has sagged and slumped
and only her ears
are unwrinkled,

though her frame is thin
as the scaffolding
that props your beans,
still she whispers softly

through her clouds
and you wonder
if it's you
she's talking to,

or if it's she
that still
has reasons to linger
and things to say.

Two Perspectives

They almost missed all two inches
of a camouflaged caterpillar
on a long, skinny leaf
so motionless they could count
the orange striations on her back.

Both wanted
to stroke her glossy jade skin,
stick their noses under the leaf
count her short, sticky legs,
hold her closer to the sun
to catch her translucence.
But they didn't.

They knew she'd soon grow on:
the boy talked about how pretty she'd be,
her patterns, bright oranges and blacks,
the fun she'd have flying,
the places she'd see.

And the grandmother wanted her to stay as she is.

A Blade of Grass

Amelia squatted
poked her head between her knees
and reached a blade of grass
her bottom grazing the ground,
the stooping unexpected because
she'd just been released from a stroller
to race her eighteen-month legs,
like a pony from a corral,
up and down a greening knoll.

Her squat was as effortless
as a grasshopper's leap,
her gaze intent as a fishing heron,
and she fingered that blade of grass
as though it were a jewel
or a rainbow bubble
touching its point, tentative,
touching over and over,
then rubbing the blade up and down
between her thumb and index finger,
brushing it against her cheek:
miracles teeming
on this old greening knoll.

A Morning with a Friend

When you hear someone say,
"this is as good as it gets,"
it gives you pause, and cause
to remember the time you landed
a feisty smallmouth bass
or moaned over Chef Pierre's
gourmet mushroom ragout.

This spring when I heard that phrase,
we were kayaking in Tarpon Bay
on a meandering narrow stream
through mangroves with roots
like stilts, embroidered with blue heron,
white ibis, and a black anhinga
who was drying out his wings.

More than the beauty of the day,
it was the pause, a comma
in the rambling weeds of a mind,
a solo of solace and peace that asked
to be noticed like a lone loon
calling in the Alaskan wilds
or the death of a beloved friend.

When Poppies Open in the Snow

In candlelight my daughter reads a poem,
her face framed by a darkened window,
hair afire, cheeks a kitchen rose,
and poppies open in the snow,
her words springing like water
pulsing from a well, their aim
true as geese who came
to listen on the roof, or the pelican
who blazes into waves for prey.
She pauses, passing the gravy, to let us see
poppies, feel the wingbeat of the geese,
worship the water, hear the pelican,
all the while coaxing out the stars.

Where Roots Echo

I finger black, loamy clumps of earth
laden with worms, richer than any soil
I've held since I lived on the other side
of this woods as a young girl.

Then I used to help my mother plant nasturtiums
around a towering bur oak that I imagined
surpassed even Jack's beanstalk,
and was the center of her black, loamy garden

along with a patch of corn that regularly
produced the first and best ears of Winnebago County,
thick and wild blackberry bushes with prickles
that would have sent Sleeping Beauty into a coma,

tree vines sturdy enough to hold a swinging
fifty-pound girl who thought she was Tarzan,
and a hilltop where she learned to love
watching and soaking in windy thunderstorms.

The old nasturtiums, and those I grow today,
are a hardy lot: ringlet tendrils stretch
toward the unknown, erupting blossoms
are simultaneously silly and sure, and

undergrowth evolves in a sea of creatures
who are cradled by the earth's marrow
as they scroll in and out of the labyrinth
there in this ground where roots echo.

About the Author

Mary Bartlett Caskey's poetry has been published most recently in *The Christian Science Monitor, Snowy Egret, Moon Journal, The Mid-America Poetry Review, Prairie Wind, The Rockford Review, Powhatan Review,* and in a *Milkweed Editions, Stories from Where We Live—The Great Lakes.* She has also won honorable mention prizes in three national poetry contests. Her poem, "A Message to the United States," has been nominated for a Pushcart Prize.

Before her retirement, she was a college administrator and a public school teacher. She lives with her husband of over fifty years in the same woods where she grew up and is the mother of three daughters and the grandmother of six. A graduate of Swarthmore College, she has worked throughout her life for the betterment of her community, Rockford, Illinois. She is a recipient of the Illinois Humanities Council's Studs Terkel Humanities Service Award and her church's Charles Parker Connolly Community Service Award. Along with poetry, she loves reading and traveling.

Printed in the United States
200044BV00011B/4-261/A